1

PART 4

ACTING (FILM & TV, STAND-UP & VOICE)

Being a professional television or film actor can

be a fulfilling yet challenging career path.

Here's a glimpse into what it's like:

1. **Variety of Roles**: You get to portray a wide range of characters, from heroes to villains, in various genres and styles of TV shows and films.

2. **Auditions**: Auditioning is a significant part of the job. You'll attend numerous auditions, often facing rejection before landing a role.

3. **Preparation**: Each role requires thorough preparation. You'll analyze the script, develop your character's backstory and motivations, and memorize lines.

4. **Collaboration**: Acting is a collaborative effort. You'll work closely with directors, fellow actors, and crew members to bring the script to life.

5. **Long Hours**: TV and film shoots can involve long hours on set, sometimes extending into late nights or early mornings.

6. **Adaptability**: You must be adaptable to changes on set, whether it's script revisions, last-minute direction, or unexpected challenges.

7. **Emotional Demands**: Some roles may require you to tap into deep emotions or portray challenging situations, which can be emotionally demanding.

8. **Public Scrutiny**: As a public figure, you may face scrutiny from fans, critics, and the media, which can sometimes be intrusive or overwhelming.

9. **Travel Opportunities**: Acting roles may take you to different locations, offering opportunities to travel and experience new places.

10. **Job Insecurity**: The industry can be unpredictable, with periods of unemployment between roles. Building a steady career requires resilience and persistence.

11. **Training and Development**: Many actors continue to train and develop their skills throughout their careers, taking classes or working with coaches to refine their craft.

12. **Financial Stability**: Income can vary significantly, especially for actors starting out. It's essential to budget and manage finances wisely during both busy and lean periods.

13. **Networking**: Building relationships with industry professionals is crucial for career advancement. Networking events, workshops, and social media can help you connect with others in the industry.

14. **Recognition and Awards**: Successful projects may lead to critical acclaim, awards recognition and increased visibility in the industry.

15. **Balance**: Balancing work and personal life can be challenging, especially during busy periods of shooting. Self-care and maintaining a support system are essential for overall well-being.

16. **Impact**: Acting allows you to entertain, inspire, and provoke thought through storytelling potentially making a positive impact on audiences.

17. **Continuous Learning**: There's always something new to learn in the ever-evolving landscape of TV and film. Staying curious and open-minded is essential for growth.

18. **Passion and Dedication**: Passion for storytelling and dedication to your craft are driving forces behind a successful acting career.

19. **Legacy**: Your work as an actor contributes to your legacy leaving behind a body of work that can inspire future generations of performers.

20. **Fulfillment**: Despite the challenges, many actors find immense fulfillment in their work knowing they're pursuing their

passion and making a meaningful contribution to the world of entertainment.

Here are 50 aspects of being a

professional TV and film actor:

1. **Auditions**: Constantly auditioning for roles, sometimes facing rejection.

2. **Memorizing Lines**: Spending time memorizing scripts.

3. **Character Development**: Developing believable characters with depth.

4. **Research**: Researching roles, backgrounds, and contexts.

5. **Training**: Continuously honing acting skills through classes and workshops.

6. **Networking**: Building connections with casting directors, agents, and other actors.

7. **Emotional Preparation**: Preparing emotionally for intense scenes.

8. **Physical Fitness**: Maintaining physical fitness for demanding roles.

9. **Dialects/Accents**: Learning and mastering various dialects and accents.

10. **Adaptability**: Being flexible and adaptable on set to changes and direction.

11. **Long Hours**: Working long hours on set, often in challenging conditions.

12. **Collaboration**: Working closely with directors, fellow actors, and crew members.

13. **Rehearsing**: Rehearsing scenes with scene partners to perfect performances.

14. **Feedback**: Being open to feedback and constructive criticism.

15. **Understanding Camera Techniques**: Understanding camera angles, framing, and movement.

16. **Continuity**: Maintaining continuity in performances across multiple takes.

17. **Wardrobe Fittings**: Attending wardrobe fittings to ensure costumes fit the character.

18. **Makeup/Hair**: Spending time in hair and makeup for character transformations.

19. **Stunts**: Performing stunts or action sequences, sometimes requiring specialized training.

20. **Script Analysis**: Analyzing scripts to understand character motivations and relationships.

21. **On-Set Etiquette**: Adhering to professional conduct and etiquette on set.

22. **Publicity**: Participating in press events, interviews, and promotional activities.

23. **Dealing with Criticism**: Handling criticism from audiences, critics, and peers.

24. **Emotional Resilience**: Developing resilience to handle the emotional toll of certain roles.

25. **Travel**: Traveling for filming locations or promotional tours.

26. **Maintaining Brand Image**: Maintaining a public persona and brand image.

27. **Balancing Personal Life**: Balancing work commitments with personal life and relationships.

28. **Financial Instability**: Facing periods of financial instability between jobs.

29. **Typecasting**: Dealing with the challenge of being typecast based on appearance or previous roles.

30. **Audience Recognition** Dealing with public recognition and privacy concerns.

31. **Creative Fulfillment**: Finding fulfillment in bringing characters to life and telling stories.

32. **Patience**: Exercising patience during the often slow-paced process of filming.

33. **Coping with Rejection**: Developing resilience to cope with rejection and uncertainty.

34. **Legal/Contractual Obligations**: Understanding and adhering to legal and contractual obligations.

35. **Personal Branding**: Building and maintaining a personal brand to attract roles and opportunities.

36. **Mental Health Awareness**: Being aware of the potential impact of acting on mental health and seeking support when needed.

37. **Continuous Learning**: Remaining curious and open to learning new skills and techniques.

38. **Industry Trends**: Keeping abreast of industry trends, technology, and changes.

39. **Cultural Sensitivity**: Being sensitive to cultural and social issues portrayed in roles.

40. **Managing Expectations**: Managing personal and professional expectations in a competitive industry.

41. **Self-Marketing**: Promoting oneself through demo reels, websites and social media.

42. **Legal Representation**: Securing legal representation to negotiate contracts and protect rights.

43. **Union Membership**: Understanding and navigating union membership and regulations.

44. **Risk-Taking**: Being willing to take creative risks and step out of comfort zones.

45. **Industry Politics**: Navigating industry politics and hierarchies.

46. **Public Speaking**: Developing public speaking skills for interviews and public appearances.

47. **Social Impact**: Recognizing the potential social impact of roles and stories portrayed.

48. **Mentorship**: Seeking mentorship from experienced actors and industry professionals.

49. **Continued Auditioning**: Continuing to audition for roles even after achieving success.

50. **Passion**: Ultimately, persevering through the challenges because of a deep love and passion for acting and storytelling.

Being a professional TV and film actor is

demanding but for many it's a deeply fulfilling

and rewarding career.

STAND-UP COMEDY

A stand-up comedian is a performer who

delivers comedic material directly to an

audience while standing on stage,

typically without the aid of costumes,

props or elaborate sets.

Stand-up comedy is a form of

entertainment where the comedian relies primarily on their spoken word, timing, delivery and stage presence to generate laughter and entertain the audience. Stand-up comedians often draw material from personal experiences, observations, social commentary, and cultural references, crafting jokes and routines that reflect their unique comedic style and perspective. The essence of stand-up comedy lies in the performer's ability to connect with the audience, elicit laughter, and engage them through witty storytelling, clever wordplay and relatable humor.

Crafting a successful stand-up comedy

act involves a blend of creativity,

performance skills, and audience

engagement.

Please remember that many stand-up

comedians have gone on to do TV & Film

so that's why we have it in regular acting

and not on it's own.

Here are 50 tips to help comedians make their stand-up comedy acts really great:

1. **Know Your Audience:** Understand the demographics and preferences of the audience you'll be performing for.

2. **Write Original Material:** Create fresh, original jokes and observations that reflect your unique perspective.

3. **Polish Your Opening:** Start with a strong, attention-grabbing joke or premise to hook the audience from the beginning.

4. **Pace Yourself:** Maintain a consistent pace throughout your set, balancing slow and fast moments for variety.

5. **Practice Timing:** Hone your comedic timing to deliver punchlines effectively and maximize laughs.

6. **Embrace Vulnerability:** Share personal stories or vulnerabilities to connect with the audience on a deeper level.

7. **Find Your Voice:** Develop a distinctive comedic voice and style that sets you apart from other comedians.

8. **Engage with the Crowd:** Interact with the audience to build rapport and create memorable moments.

9. **Use Callbacks:** Refer back to earlier jokes or moments in your set to create callbacks and tie your material together.

10. **Stay Relevant:** Keep your material current and relevant to the times to resonate with modern audiences.

11. **Mix Up Topics:** Cover a range of topics and themes to keep your set dynamic and engaging.

12. **Practice Self-Editing:** Cut out unnecessary words or details to streamline your jokes and make them more impactful.

13. **Craft Strong Transitions:** Smoothly transition between jokes and segments to maintain flow and momentum.

14. **Emphasize Visuals:** Use physical gestures, facial expressions, and body language to enhance your delivery.

15. **Experiment with Tone:** Play with different tones – from silly and absurd to dry and observational – to keep your set diverse.

16. **Work on Stage Presence:** Develop a confident and commanding stage presence that captivates the audience.

17. **Study Comedy Masters:** Learn from seasoned comedians by watching their performances and analyzing their techniques.

18. **Stay Authentic:** Be true to yourself and your comedic sensibilities rather than trying to emulate others.

19. **Seek Feedback:** Solicit feedback from peers, mentors, and audience members to refine your material and delivery.

20. **Stay Flexible:** Be prepared to adapt your set on the fly based on audience reactions and the vibe of the room.

21. **Record Performances:** Record your performances to review later and identify areas for improvement.

22. **Create a Strong Closer:** End your set with a memorable and impactful joke or statement that leaves a lasting impression.

23. **Maintain Energy:** Keep your energy levels high throughout your set to keep the audience engaged and entertained.

24. **Rehearse Out Loud:** Practice your set out loud to refine your delivery and timing.

25. **Use Silence:** Embrace moments of silence for comedic effect, allowing punchlines to land and build anticipation.

26. **Stay Positive:** Keep a positive attitude on stage, even if a joke doesn't land as expected.

27. **Stay in the Moment:** Stay present and focused on the current joke or interaction rather than getting ahead of yourself.

28. **Be Observant:** Pay attention to your surroundings and incorporate current events or audience reactions into your set.

29. **Stay Persistent:** Keep performing regularly and refining your material over time to grow as a comedian.

30. **Find Your Niche:** Identify topics or themes that resonate with your comedic voice and explore them in depth.

31. **Learn from Bombing:** Embrace bombing as a learning experience and an opportunity to grow as a comedian.

32. **Use Contrast:** Incorporate contrast in your set by mixing light-hearted humor with moments of depth or introspection.

33. **Experiment with Delivery:** Try experimenting with different accents, voices, or personas to add variety to your performance.

34. **Stay Relevant:** Stay up-to-date with current trends, pop culture references, and societal issues to keep your material fresh.

35. **Develop a Strong Opener:** Start your set with a joke or observation that immediately grabs the audience's attention and sets the tone for your performance.

36. **Use the Rule of Three:** Employ the rule of three in your jokes by presenting a series of items or ideas followed by a punchline or twist on the third item.

37. **Embrace the Unexpected:** Embrace unexpected moments or interruptions as opportunities for improvisation and spontaneous humor.

38. **Work on Timing:** Perfect your timing by practicing delivery and pauses to maximize the impact of your punchlines.

39. **Be Confident in Silence:** Don't rush through your set; embrace pauses and silence to let jokes sink in and build tension.

40. **Stay Relatable:** Connect with the audience by sharing relatable experiences and observations that resonate with their own lives.

41. **Stay in Control:** Maintain control of the stage and audience by projecting confidence and authority in your delivery.

42. **Be Authentic:** Be true to yourself and your comedic voice; avoid trying to imitate other comedians or forcing a persona that isn't genuine.

43. **Practice Empathy:** Consider the perspective of your audience and tailor your material to their sensibilities and tastes.

44. **End on a High Note:** Finish your set with a strong closing joke or call-back that leaves the audience laughing and wanting more.

45. **Create a Memorable Catchphrase:** Introduce a catchphrase or recurring joke that becomes associated with your act and helps you stand out in the minds of audiences.

46. **Engage with the Audience:** Interact with audience members to create moments of spontaneity and connection that enhance the overall experience.

47. **Use Visual Aids:** Incorporate props, visual aids, or multimedia elements into your act to add visual interest and enhance comedic impact.

48. **Be Vulnerable:** Don't be afraid to share personal anecdotes or vulnerabilities that add depth and authenticity to your performance.

49. **Take Risks:** Experiment with new material, styles, or techniques to push the boundaries of your comedy and keep your act fresh and exciting.

50. **Have Fun:** Above all, enjoy yourself on stage and let your passion for comedy shine through; when you're having fun, the audience will too!

By incorporating these tips and techniques into their stand-up comedy acts, comedians can enhance their performances, connect more deeply with audiences, and stand out in the competitive world of comedy.

SINGING

A professional singer is someone who earns a living by performing vocal music professionally. They typically have developed their singing skills through training and practice and they may perform in a variety of settings such as concerts, stage productions, recording studios or even television and film.

Professional singers often work with agents or managers to secure gigs and contracts, and they may collaborate with other musicians or songwriters to create and perform music.

They may specialize in a particular genre such as classical, pop, rock, jazz, or opera, or they may have a diverse repertoire.

Overall, a professional singer is someone who is dedicated to their craft and earns income through their singing abilities.

Here are 20 steps you can take to pursue a career as a professional singer:

1. **Take vocal lessons:** Invest in vocal training with a qualified vocal coach to develop proper singing technique, range, control, and breath support.

2. **Identify your vocal style:** Discover your unique vocal style and genre preferences, whether it's pop, rock, jazz, classical, R&B, country, or another genre.

3. **Practice regularly:** Dedicate time to daily vocal exercises and practice sessions to improve your vocal skills, range, and stamina.

4. **Learn music theory:** Gain a basic understanding of music theory, including notes, scales, chords, and rhythm, to enhance your musical knowledge and communication with other musicians.

5. **Expand your repertoire:** Learn a diverse selection of songs across different genres to showcase your versatility as a singer.

6. **Perform live:** Gain performance experience by singing at local venues, open mic nights, talent shows, or community events to develop your stage presence and confidence.

7. **Record demos:** Create demo recordings of your singing to showcase your talent and style to potential collaborators, producers, and record labels.

8. **Build a strong online presence:** Establish a professional website and social media profiles to showcase your music, connect with fans, and attract industry attention.

9. **Collaborate with other musicians:** Collaborate with songwriters, composers, and other musicians to create original music or cover songs and expand your musical network.

10. **Join a choir or vocal group:** Participate in a choir, vocal ensemble, or acapella group to improve your vocal skills, harmony, and performance abilities in a group setting.

11. **Attend workshops and masterclasses:** Take advantage of workshops, masterclasses, and vocal coaching sessions conducted by experienced singers and industry professionals to learn new techniques and gain insights into the music industry.

12. **Seek feedback:** Be open to constructive criticism from vocal coaches, peers, and industry professionals to identify areas for improvement and refine your singing technique.

13. **Audition for singing competitions:** Audition for singing competitions and talent shows to gain exposure, receive feedback from judges, and showcase your talent to a wider audience.

14. **Promote yourself:** Actively promote your music and performances through social media, press releases, email newsletters, and networking events to attract fans and industry attention.

15. **Build a professional team:** Surround yourself with a team of professionals, including a manager, agent, publicist, and legal

advisor, to help you navigate the music industry and advance your career.

16. **Create a press kit:** Develop a professional press kit that includes your bio, photos, videos, press clippings, and contact information to present to industry contacts, venues, and media outlets.

17. **Secure gigs:** Book live performances at music venues, clubs, festivals, weddings, corporate events, and other opportunities to showcase your talent and gain exposure.

18. **Invest in quality recordings:** Record high-quality demos or studio albums with experienced producers and engineers to showcase your best performances and attract industry attention.

19. **Network:** Attend music industry events, conferences, showcases, and networking mixers to connect with other musicians, producers, songwriters, and industry professionals.

20. **Stay persistent and resilient:** Be prepared for rejection and setbacks along the way, but remain committed to your passion for singing and continue to pursue your goals with determination and resilience.

By following these steps and remaining

dedicated to your craft, you can work towards

becoming a professional singer and achieving

success in the music industry.

DANCING

Becoming a professional dancer takes

dedication, talent and perseverance.

Here are 20 steps you can take to pursue a career in dance:

1. **Take dance classes:** Start by enrolling in dance classes to learn different styles and techniques. Choose a reputable dance studio or school with experienced instructors.

2. **Train intensively:** Dedicate yourself to regular, consistent training to improve your skills and technique. Practice various dance styles to broaden your abilities.

3. **Study different dance styles:** Explore a range of dance styles such as ballet, jazz, contemporary, hip-hop, tap, or ballroom to diversify your skill set.

4. **Attend workshops and masterclasses:** Participate in workshops and masterclasses conducted by renowned dancers and choreographers to gain new insights and techniques.

5. **Get formal education:** Consider pursuing a degree or diploma in dance from a performing arts school or university to receive structured training and education in dance theory.

6. **Build strength and flexibility:** Focus on conditioning exercises to build strength, flexibility, and endurance, which are essential for dancers to perform at their best and prevent injuries.

7. **Develop performance skills:** Work on expressing emotions and storytelling through dance, as well as stage presence and charisma, to captivate audiences during performances.

8. **Seek feedback:** Be open to constructive criticism from instructors, choreographers, and peers to identify areas for improvement and grow as a dancer.

9. **Audition for dance companies:** Audition for dance companies, dance productions, or performance groups to gain professional experience and exposure.

10. **Create a dance reel:** Compile videos of your dance performances and choreography to showcase your skills and versatility to potential employers or collaborators.

11. **Network:** Attend dance events, competitions, and industry gatherings to network with other dancers, choreographers, and industry professionals.

12. **Collaborate with other artists:** Collaborate with musicians, composers, filmmakers, and other artists to create interdisciplinary performances and expand your creative horizons.

13. **Perform in showcases:** Participate in dance showcases, festivals, and community events to gain visibility and build your reputation as a dancer.

14. **Stay informed:** Keep up-to-date with current trends, developments, and opportunities in the dance industry through dance publications, websites, and social media.

15. **Seek mentorship:** Find mentors who can offer guidance, support, and advice as you navigate your dance career path.

16. **Stay disciplined:** Maintain a disciplined practice routine, set goals for yourself, and stay motivated to continuously improve and progress as a dancer.

17. **Audition for dance competitions:** Participate in dance competitions to challenge yourself, gain exposure, and receive recognition for your talent and skill.

18. **Consider teaching dance:** Explore opportunities to teach dance classes or workshops to share your knowledge and passion for dance with others while supplementing your income.

19. **Stay healthy:** Take care of your body by eating a balanced diet, staying hydrated, getting enough rest, and seeking medical attention when necessary to prevent injuries and maintain peak performance.

20. **Persevere:** Be resilient and persistent in pursuing your dreams of becoming a professional dancer, even in the face of challenges and setbacks.

Believe in yourself and your abilities, and

never give up on your passion for dance.

OFF-CAMERA:

VOICEOVERS

Voice Over Narrators typically focus on the following types of projects:

- Audiobooks

- Documentaries

- Explainer videos

- Educational videos

- Business videos

- Medical videos

- Audio tour guides

Voiceover artists rely on their vocal abilities to convey emotions, portray characters, and deliver messages effectively. Here are five voice exercises specifically tailored for voiceover artists to warm up, strengthen, and improve their vocal performance:

1. **Breathing exercises:**

- Diaphragmatic breathing: Stand or sit comfortably and place one hand on your chest and the other on your abdomen. Inhale deeply through your nose, allowing your abdomen to expand as you fill your lungs with air.

Exhale slowly through your mouth, feeling your abdomen contract. Repeat several times to strengthen your diaphragm and improve breath control.

- Straw breathing: Take a straw and place it between your lips. Inhale deeply through the straw, focusing on maintaining a steady airflow. Exhale slowly through the straw, controlling the airflow with your abdominal muscles. This exercise helps to regulate your breath and warm up your vocal cords.

2. **Vocal warm-up exercises:**

- Lip trills: Relax your lips and blow air through them, creating a buzzing sound. Start with a low pitch and gradually move to a higher pitch, maintaining a smooth and steady vibration. This exercise helps to relax and warm up your lips, tongue, and vocal cords.

- Humming scales: Humming scales or sirens on different pitches helps to loosen up your vocal cords, improve vocal flexibility, and warm up your voice for speaking or singing.

3. **Articulation exercises:**

- Tongue twisters: Practice tongue twisters such as "Peter Piper picked a peck of pickled peppers" or "She sells seashells by the seashore" to improve your articulation, diction, and clarity of speech. Repeat each tongue twister several times, gradually increasing your speed while maintaining accuracy.

- Vowel exercises: Pronounce each vowel sound (A, E, I, O, U) clearly and distinctly, holding each sound for a few seconds. Focus on maintaining a relaxed jaw, tongue, and throat while producing each vowel sound.

4. **Resonance exercises:**

- Nasal and oral resonance: Alternate between producing sounds with nasal resonance (such as "ng" or "mmm") and oral resonance (such as

"ah" or "oo") to explore different vocal resonators and improve vocal clarity and projection.

- Vocal sirens: Glide smoothly between your lowest and highest vocal pitches, exaggerating the movement of your voice up and down like a siren.

This exercise helps to expand your vocal range, improve vocal resonance, and reduce vocal strain.

5. **Characterization exercises:**

- Character voice warm-up: Warm up your voice while

practicing specific character voices or accents relevant to upcoming voiceover projects. Focus on capturing the tone, pitch, rhythm, and mannerisms of each character to bring them to life effectively.

- Script reading: Practice reading scripts aloud with different vocal tones, emotions, and pacing to develop versatility in your voice and acting skills. Experiment with conveying various emotions, such as excitement, sadness, anger, or humor, to effectively convey the message of the script.

Consistently practicing these voice exercises can help voiceover artists maintain vocal health, improve vocal technique, and enhance their performance skills for a variety of voiceover projects.

VOICE ACTORS

Voice Actors can be found lending their

voices to:

- Animated movies

- TV cartoons

- Radio dramas

- ADR (Automated Dialog Replacement)

- Video games

• Puppet shows

• Foreign language dubbing

Getting into character as a voice actor is essential for delivering authentic and compelling performances. Here are five effective ways to immerse yourself in a character's mindset:

1. **Character analysis:**

- Start by thoroughly analyzing the character you're portraying. Understand their backstory, personality traits, motivations, and emotional journey within the script. Consider factors such as age, gender, background, and any unique quirks or characteristics that define the character.

- Ask yourself questions like: What drives this character? What are their fears, desires, and conflicts? How do they speak and move? The more you understand the character, the better you can embody them in your performance.

2. **Emotional preparation:**

- Connect with the character's emotions and experiences on a personal level. Draw from your own life experiences and emotions to empathize with the character's feelings and reactions.

- Use relaxation techniques, visualization, or method acting exercises to evoke and channel the appropriate emotions for the character. This emotional authenticity will shine through in your voice performance.

3. **Vocal exploration:**

- Experiment with your voice to find the right vocal qualities and nuances for the character.

Adjust your pitch, tone, pace, rhythm, and accent to match the character's age, personality, and background.

- Practice vocal warm-up exercises to prepare your voice for the demands of the character's voice, whether it's a high-energy cartoon character, a wise elder, or a smooth-talking narrator.

4. **Physical embodiment:**

- Physically embodying the character can help you inhabit their persona more fully. Stand or sit in a way that reflects the character's posture, gestures, and physicality.

- Use facial expressions, hand movements, and body language to convey the character's emotions and actions. This physical engagement can enhance the authenticity and expressiveness of your voice performance.

5. **Contextual immersion:**

- Immerse yourself in the world of the script or project to better understand the context and dynamics of the character's environment. Familiarize yourself with the setting, time period, culture, and relationships depicted in the story.

- Imagine yourself living in the character's world and interacting with other characters and elements of the story. This contextual understanding will inform your interpretation of the character and enrich your performance with depth and realism.

By incorporating these techniques into your

preparation process, you can effectively get into

character as a voice actor and deliver compelling

performances that resonate with audiences.

Things you will need:

THEATRICAL HEADSHOTS

**A theatrical headshot is a type of photograph
specifically tailored for actors seeking roles in
theater, film, television, and other dramatic productions.
Unlike commercial headshots, which aim to
present actors in a friendly and relatable manner
suited for advertising and marketing campaigns,**

theatrical headshots are designed to convey the

actor's range, personality and ability to embody

different characters and emotions.

Key features of theatrical headshots include:

1. **Character and Emotion**: Theatrical headshots often showcase a range of expressions, from serious and intense to light-hearted and playful, depending on the actor's casting range.

2. **Dramatic Lighting**: Lighting in theatrical headshots may be more dramatic or moody to create depth and emphasize the actor's facial features and expressions.

3. **Backdrop and Environment**: The background in theatrical headshots may be more varied and dynamic, reflecting the diverse settings and genres of theater, film, and television productions. It could range from neutral backgrounds to scenic locations or urban landscapes.

4. **Wardrobe Choices**: Actors may wear clothing in theatrical headshots that reflect the types of roles they typically audition for, whether it's period costumes, business attire, casual wear, or character-specific costumes.

5. **Characterization**: Theatrical headshots may incorporate subtle props or accessories to help convey the actor's ability to inhabit specific characters or roles.

6. **Eye Direction**: Actors may direct their gaze away from the camera in theatrical headshots to suggest thoughtfulness, introspection, or engagement with another character or scene.

7. **Posture and Body Language**: The actor's posture and body language in theatrical headshots may vary depending on the characters they portray, from confident and assertive to vulnerable or subdued.

Theatrical headshots are an essential tool for actors to showcase their versatility, talent, and suitability for a wide range of dramatic roles.

They serve as the actor's calling card and are often submitted to casting directors, agents, and production companies when auditioning for theater, film, television, and other performance opportunities.

COMEDY HEADSHOT

A comedy actor headshot should capture your personality, energy, and sense of humor while still maintaining a professional appearance.

Here are some tips for creating a great comedy actor headshot:

1. **Expressive Facial Expression**: Choose a facial expression that reflects your comedic style and personality. It could be a smile, a smirk, a raised eyebrow, or a playful expression that showcases your sense of humor.

2. **Warmth and Approachability**: Aim for a headshot that exudes warmth and approachability, inviting casting directors and audiences to connect with you on a personal level. A genuine and friendly expression can make you more relatable and likable.

3. **Natural Lighting**: Opt for natural lighting or soft studio lighting that enhances your features and creates a flattering look. Avoid harsh shadows or overly dramatic lighting that can distract from your expression.

4. **Simple Background**: Choose a clean and simple background that doesn't distract from your face. Neutral colors like white, gray, or light blue are often preferred as they allow the focus to remain on you.

5. **Wardrobe Choice**: Select wardrobe options that reflect your comedic persona and personal style. Whether it's a colorful shirt, a quirky accessory, or a fun prop, your outfit should complement your character without overshadowing it.

6. **Head and Shoulders Shot**: The focus of a headshot should be on your face, so aim for a head and shoulders shot that frames your face nicely without cutting off any important features.

7. **Multiple Looks**: Consider including a variety of expressions and poses in your comedy actor headshot session. This allows you to showcase different facets of your personality and comedic range, giving casting directors a better sense of your versatility.

8. **Professional Quality**: Invest in a professional photographer who specializes in headshot photography and understands the unique requirements of comedy actor headshots. A high-quality image can make a significant difference in how you are perceived by industry professionals.

9. **Authenticity**: Above all, aim to capture your authentic self in your comedy actor headshot.

Let your personality shine through and don't be afraid to show off your natural quirks and humor.

Remember, your comedy actor headshot is often the first impression you make on casting directors and agents so make sure it accurately represents who you are as a performer and leaves a lasting impact.

YOUR "REEL"

Having a good reel as an actor is

incredibly important. Your reel serves as your visual calling card, showcasing your range, talent and versatility to casting directors, agents, managers and other industry professionals.

The Power of a Strong Acting Reel

Your acting reel is like your calling card in the entertainment industry. It's often the first impression you make, so it needs to be strong. A well-crafted reel can: 1. Demonstrate your ability to embody different characters, emotions, and acting styles 2. Help secure auditions and roles by showing decision-makers that you're a good fit for specific projects

The Importance of an Online Presence

In today's digital age, where online platforms play a significant role in casting processes, your reel can also:

1. Be easily shared and viewed by industry insiders around the world This global accessibility makes it even more essential to have a polished and professional reel that effectively highlights your strengths.

The Impact on Your Acting Career

Ultimately, a good reel can significantly enhance your chances of: 1. Getting noticed by casting directors and agents

2. Landing acting opportunities

So investing time and effort into creating one is definitely worthwhile.

MAIN REEL (Showcasing all different abilities)

Creating a standout acting

reel requires careful selection

of scenes and attention to

detail.

Here are 50 things actors can do to

make their dramatic acting reel truly

exceptional:

1. Choose scenes that showcase your range and versatility as an actor.

2. Select scenes with strong emotional content and character development.

3. Ensure that each scene has a clear beginning, middle, and end.

4. Include a variety of scenes that demonstrate different genres and styles of drama.

5. Edit your reel to highlight your best moments and performances.

6. Keep the reel concise, ideally between 2 to 3 minutes in length.

7. Start with a strong opening scene to grab the viewer's attention.

8. Use high-quality footage with clear audio and visuals.

9. Incorporate professional editing techniques to enhance the overall presentation.

10. Consider using music to set the tone and mood of the reel.

11. Include a diverse range of characters, ages, and demographics in your scenes.

12. Showcase your ability to convey complex emotions through facial expressions and body language.

13. Pay attention to continuity and consistency between scenes.

14. Ensure that each scene contributes to the overall narrative and theme of the reel.

15. Include scenes that highlight your ability to carry a scene as the lead or supporting actor.

16. Avoid using scenes with distracting background noise or visual elements.

17. Show your ability to perform under different lighting conditions and settings.

18. Incorporate scenes that feature strong dialogue and dynamic interactions with other characters.

19. Choose scenes that allow you to demonstrate your ability to handle intense or challenging subject matter.

20. Consider including scenes that showcase your physicality and action skills, if applicable.

21. Show your range by including scenes with different pacing and intensity levels.

22. Incorporate scenes that highlight your ability to improvise and react in the moment.

23. Include scenes that showcase your ability to convey internal conflict and turmoil.

24. Pay attention to the order of scenes to create a cohesive and engaging narrative flow.

25. Include a mix of close-up shots, medium shots, and wide shots to vary the visual presentation.

26. Showcase your ability to convey subtle emotions and nuances through your performance.

27. Consider including scenes that showcase your ability to speak different languages or accents.

28. Incorporate scenes that highlight your ability to portray characters from different time periods or cultures.

29. Show your range by including scenes with different levels of character transformation or growth.

30. Use scenes that allow you to demonstrate your ability to handle complex dialogue and monologues.

31. Include scenes that showcase your ability to convey emotion through physical actions and gestures.

32. Choose scenes that allow you to showcase your chemistry with other actors.

33. Consider including scenes that showcase your comedic timing and sense of humor, if appropriate.

34. Pay attention to the pacing of the reel to keep the viewer engaged from start to finish.

35. Show your ability to convey emotion through subtle changes in facial expression and body language.

36. Incorporate scenes that showcase your ability to convey vulnerability and authenticity.

37. Use scenes that feature strong conflict and tension to create dramatic impact.

38. Consider including scenes that showcase your ability to handle complex character relationships.

39. Include scenes that showcase your ability to handle emotional and physical challenges.

40. Show your ability to convey a character's inner thoughts and motivations through your performance.

41. Pay attention to the quality of the acting in each scene, and choose scenes where your performance shines.

42. Include a variety of scenes that demonstrate your ability to play different types of characters.

43. Show your ability to handle challenging material with sensitivity and depth.

44. Choose scenes that allow you to demonstrate your range as an actor, from subtle to intense performances.

45. Use scenes that showcase your ability to convey emotion through your eyes and facial expressions.

46. Pay attention to the pacing and rhythm of the reel, and edit it to keep the viewer engaged throughout.

47. Include scenes that showcase your ability to handle both dramatic and comedic material, if applicable.

48. Show your ability to create fully realized characters with depth and complexity.

49. Choose scenes that leave a lasting impression on the viewer and make them want to see more.

50. Finally, always strive for authenticity and honesty in your performances, as these are the qualities that will truly resonate with viewers.

COMEDY REEL (Separate from main reel)

Creating a standout comedy acting reel requires a mix of talent, creativity and strategy.

Here are 50 tips to make your comedy acting reel really great:
1. **Choose Strong Material:** Select scenes or sketches that showcase your comedic strengths and range.

2. **Keep it Short:** Aim for a reel that's around 2-3 minutes long to maintain viewer engagement.

3. **Open with a Bang:** Start with your strongest and most attention-grabbing clip.

4. **Showcase Versatility:** Include a variety of comedic styles and characters to demonstrate range.

5. **Highlight Timing:** Choose scenes that showcase your impeccable comedic timing.

6. **Embrace Physical Comedy:** Include physical humor and slapstick elements if they highlight your skills.

7. **Include Memorable Characters:** Feature characters with distinct personalities and quirks.

8. **Mix Dialogue and Monologue:** Include both dialogue-driven scenes and monologues to showcase different skills.

9. **Feature Reactions:** Include clips that highlight your ability to react and play off other actors.

10. **Focus on Chemistry:** Include scenes where you have strong chemistry with scene partners.

11. **Cut to the Punchline:** Keep scenes concise and cut out any unnecessary setup to get to the punchline quickly.

12. **Avoid Excessive Exposition:** Choose scenes that don't require extensive backstory or setup to understand.

13. **Incorporate Improv:** If you excel at improv include a clip that showcases your spontaneous wit.

14. **Use High-Quality Footage:** Ensure that the video and audio quality of each clip is top-notch.

15. **Edit with Precision:** Use seamless editing transitions to keep the reel flowing smoothly.

16. **Include a Variety of Settings:** Showcase your ability to perform comedy in different environments and scenarios.

17. **Feature Recognizable Material:** Include scenes from well-known comedies or parodies if appropriate.

18. **Add a Title Card:** Introduce yourself with a professional title card at the beginning of the reel.

19. **Include Contact Information:** Ensure your contact information is easily accessible at the end of the reel.

20. **Inject Personality:** Let your unique personality shine through in each clip.

21. **Choose Memorable Lines:** Include lines or catchphrases that are memorable and quotable.

22. **Consider Montages:** Create a montage of quick, comedic moments if appropriate for your style.

23. **Showcase Character Transformations:** Include clips that demonstrate your ability to transform into different characters.

24. **Use Music Wisely:** Choose background music that complements the tone of each scene without overshadowing your performance.

25. **End on a High Note:** Close the reel with another strong clip to leave a lasting impression.

26. **Get Feedback:** Share your reel with trusted friends, mentors, or industry professionals for constructive feedback.

27. **Trim the Fat:** Cut out any scenes or moments that don't contribute to showcasing your comedic talents.

28. **Keep it Current:** Regularly update your reel with fresh material to reflect your growth as a performer.

29. **Tailor to Your Brand:** Ensure that the overall tone and content of the reel align with your comedic brand and casting goals.

30. **Inject Energy:** Infuse each clip with energy and enthusiasm to keep viewers engaged.

31. **Consider Group Scenes:** If applicable, include scenes where you shine in group dynamics and ensemble comedy.

32. **Show Facial Expressions:** Highlight your facial expressions and reactions to enhance the comedic impact.

33. **Experiment with Props:** Use props creatively to enhance the humor of certain scenes.

34. **Explore Parody:** Include scenes that parody recognizable characters or genres if it fits your style.

35. **Create a Strong Opening Line:** Start each scene with a memorable and attention-grabbing line or action.

36. **Incorporate Visual Gags:** Include visual humor and sight gags to add depth to your reel.

37. **Stay Authentic:** Showcase your authentic comedic voice and style rather than trying to mimic others.

38. **Play with Expectations:** Subvert expectations or play with comedic conventions to keep viewers engaged.

39. **Maintain Consistency:** Ensure that the tone and style of each clip flow cohesively throughout the reel.

40. **Include Crowd Pleasers:** If you have clips that consistently get laughs from audiences, prioritize including them.

41. **Create a Narrative Arc:** Arrange clips in a way that creates a narrative or emotional arc for the viewer.

42. **Inject Surprises:** Include unexpected twists or punchlines to keep viewers on their toes.

43. **Avoid Dated References:** Choose material that will remain relevant and timeless, avoiding overly dated pop culture references.

44. **Be Selective:** Quality over quantity – prioritize including fewer high-quality clips rather than overcrowding the reel.

45. **Consider Web Series Clips:** If you've appeared in comedic web series, include clips that showcase your work.

46. **Include Bloopers or Outtakes:** Add a blooper reel at the end for a lighthearted touch, if appropriate.

47. **Think About Sequencing:** Arrange clips in a way that creates a natural flow and progression of humor.

48. **Research Industry Standards:** Familiarize yourself with industry standards for comedy reels and adjust accordingly.

49. **Stay Professional:** Maintain a professional demeanor and tone throughout the reel.

50. **Have Fun:** Let your passion for comedy shine through and enjoy the process of creating your reel!

By incorporating these tips and techniques, you can create a comedy acting reel

that effectively showcases your talents, grabs attention, and leaves a lasting

impression on casting directors and industry professionals.

Audition Techniques

Here are 50 professional audition techniques for new

actors and yes maybe even a few of you veterans.

**Remember that this is a marathon & not a sprint. Pace
yourself:)**

Be patient with yourself:)

1. **Research the Role**: Understand the character you're
auditioning for, their background, and motivations.

2. **Learn the Script**: Memorize your lines or shoot and understand the context behind them.

3. **Develop the Character**: Create a backstory for your character to bring depth to your performance.

4. **Practice Cold Reading**: Train yourself to read and perform lines without prior rehearsal.

5. **Work on Monologues**: Have a few monologues prepared to showcase your range and versatility.

6. **Physical Warm-up**: Stretch and warm up your body before auditions to avoid stiffness.

7. **Vocal Warm-up**: Practice vocal exercises to ensure clarity and projection.

8. **Breathing Exercises**: Control your breathing to maintain composure and support your voice.

9. **Focus on Eye Contact**: Maintain eye contact with the casting director or reader to establish connection.

10. **Listen Actively**: Pay attention to instructions and feedback during the audition process.

11. **Stay in Character**: Remain in character from the moment you enter the audition room until you leave.

12. **Use Props Wisely**: If allowed, use props to enhance your performance, but don't rely on them.

13. **Be Flexible**: Be prepared to take direction and adapt your performance accordingly.

14. **Embrace Nerves**: Use nervous energy to fuel your performance rather than letting it hinder you.

15. **Dress Appropriately**: Wear attire that fits the character and is professional yet comfortable.

16. **Arrive Early**: Show up with plenty of time to spare to avoid rushing and feeling flustered.

17. **Be Polite and Professional**: Treat everyone you encounter with respect, from the receptionist to the casting director.

18. **Bring Headshots and Resumes**: Have copies of your headshot and resume to leave with casting directors.

19. **Stay Positive**: Maintain a positive attitude even if things don't go as planned.

20. **Network**: Build relationships with casting directors, agents, and other industry professionals.

21. **Seek Feedback**: Don't be afraid to ask for feedback to improve your auditioning skills.

22. **Record Yourself**: Record your auditions to review and critique your performance.

23. **Take Acting Classes**: Continuously hone your craft through acting classes and workshops.

24. **Study Different Techniques**: Explore various acting techniques to find what works best for you.

25. **Be Yourself**: Let your personality shine through in your audition while still staying true to the character.

26. **Research the Casting Director**: Learn about the casting director's preferences and past projects.

27. **Follow Instructions Carefully**: Pay close attention to audition guidelines and follow them precisely.

28. **Prepare Questions**: Have thoughtful questions prepared to ask after your audition, if appropriate.

29. **Stay Hydrated**: Drink water to keep your voice and body hydrated.

30. **Practice Relaxation Techniques**: Incorporate relaxation techniques like meditation or deep breathing to calm nerves.

31. **Visualize Success**: Picture yourself delivering a successful audition before entering the room.

32. **Maintain Good Posture**: Stand tall and confident to exude presence and poise.

33. **Project Confidence**: Even if you're nervous, project confidence in your abilities.

34. **Be Versatile**: Showcase your range by auditioning for a variety of roles.

35. **Stay Informed**: Keep up with industry trends and developments to stay relevant.

36. **Show Emotional Range**: Demonstrate your ability to convey a range of emotions authentically.

37. **Be Memorable**: Find ways to make your audition stand out without being gimmicky.

38. **Stay Grounded**: Don't let success or rejection define your worth as an actor or model.

39. **Work on Improvisation Skills**: Practice improvisation to think on your feet during auditions.

40. **Build Confidence**: Build confidence in yourself and your abilities through preparation and practice.

41. **Seek Support**: Surround yourself with a supportive network of friends, family, and mentors.

42. **Stay Persistent**: Rejection is part of the industry, so keep auditioning and improving.

43. **Keep Learning**: Continuously seek opportunities to learn and grow as an actor or model.

44. **Stay Healthy**: Take care of your physical and mental health to sustain a long and fulfilling career.

45. **Be Authentic**: Authenticity resonates with casting directors and audiences alike.

46. **Stay Updated on Industry Events**: Attend industry events and network with fellow professionals.

47. **Be Grateful**: Express gratitude for every opportunity, big or small.

48. **Have a Backup Plan**: While pursuing your passion, have a backup plan to support yourself financially.

49. **Celebrate Small Wins**: Acknowledge and celebrate your achievements along the way.

50. **Never Stop Dreaming**: Stay true to your dreams and never give up on pursuing them.

"Please remember that each audition is a chance to learn

and grow so approach them with enthusiasm and a

willingness to improve"

GOOD LUCK!!!!

BUSINESS TIPS!! ALERT! ALERT!

"ACROSS THE BOARDS"

Please be *very careful* of agencies that say "We want to sign you across the boards" when you are new.

First of all, "across the boards" means that an agency or management company

would like to sign the talent to a one or two year exclusive contract in the print(modeling), commercial & theatrical(meaning TV & FILM)departments.

Sounds exciting right?? This is basically a sales tactic and quite honestly the

talent are nowhere near ready. They aren't ready and they're not packaged

properly to go in front of casting for TV & Film. The agency doesn't have to say

much really because they just let the talent assume that they are going to do

something for them theatrically.

The talent also doesn't say anything because they don't want to rock the boat &

99% of them wind up in an ocean of talent in the print & commercial department

locked into a 1 or 2 year contract.

Hmmmmm!! Now What???

But Wait! There IS more actually!

They tell them this because they like them for modeling & commercials and feel

they can make money off them. In all reality it is the way agencies make a living

unless they are one of the big agencies.

The way you keep this in check is to have a company only represent you for modeling & commercials and go with a management company or agency that

only does theatrical(TV & Film)& doesn't even have a commercial or

print(modeling)department.

This way it keeps it honest & lets face it, if you're good enough theatrically(TV &

FILM)then someone will see you and approach you BECAUSE THEY WILL WANT

TO MAKE MONEY OFF YOU.

LET'S FACE IT! EITHER SOMEBODY HAS IT OR THEY DON'T

AND LUCK EVENTUALLY RUNS OUT BECAUSE YOU MUST BE

GOOD AT THE CRAFT!!!

Just keep honing the craft (acting class, plays,

student films, shorts, small independent films

& so on) & they will come!!

RESIDUALS

What Are Residuals?

Residuals are additional payments made to

actors, writers, directors and other talent for

the reuse or rebroadcast of their work beyond

the initial airing or release. In the context of

film and television, residuals typically refer to

payments made to performers for subsequent

uses of their work, such as reruns,

syndication, foreign distribution, home video

sales and digital streaming.

Here's a breakdown of what residuals from film and television encompass: 1. **Rerun Residuals**: When a television show or film is rebroadcast or syndicated on television, performers are entitled to residuals based on the number of reruns and the market in which they air.

2. **Foreign Residuals**: Residuals are paid when a television show or film is aired in international markets. The amount may vary depending on the distribution territory and the terms of the actor's contract.

3. **Home Video Residuals**: When a television show or film is sold or rented on physical media such as DVD, Blu-ray, or VHS, performers receive residuals based on a percentage of the revenue generated from those sales or rentals.

4. **New Media Residuals**: With the rise of digital streaming platforms like Netflix, Hulu and Amazon Prime performers are entitled to residuals when their work is streamed online. New media residuals are typically governed by separate agreements from traditional television and film residuals.

5. **Clip Usage Residuals**: Performers may also receive residuals for the use of clips from their work in various contexts, such as commercials, documentaries or news programs.

ANOTHER LOOK AT IT:)

Residuals: Ensuring Ongoing Compensation for Actors

Residuals are an important aspect of compensation for actors in television and film ensuring ongoing payment

for their work beyond the initial airing or release of a project.

Here are 20 things actors should know about television and film residuals: 1. **Definition**: Residuals are additional payments made to actors for the reuse or rebroadcast of their work beyond the initial airing or release.

2. **Union Regulations**: Residuals are typically governed by union agreements such as SAG-AFTRA (Screen Actors Guild-American Federation of Television and Radio Artists) for actors in the United States.

3. **Types of Residuals**: There are various types of residuals, including rerun residuals, foreign residuals, home video residuals and new media residuals (for streaming platforms).

4. **Formula for Calculating Residuals**: Residuals are calculated based on a formula that takes into account factors such as the type of use, the media market and the actor's contract.

5. **Initial Payment vs. Residuals**: Actors typically receive an initial payment for their work upfront with residuals providing additional income over time.

6. **Rerun Residuals**: Rerun residuals are paid when a television show or film is rebroadcast or syndicated on television.

7. **Foreign Residuals**: Foreign residuals are paid when a television show or film is aired in international markets.

8. **Home Video Residuals**: Home video residuals are paid when a television show or film is sold or rented on DVD, Blu-ray or other physical media.

9. **New Media Residuals**: New media residuals are paid when a television show or film is streamed on platforms such as Netflix, Hulu or Amazon Prime.

10. **Minimum Compensation**: Union agreements establish minimum rates and conditions for residuals, ensuring actors receive fair compensation for their work.

11. **Distribution Windows**: Residuals are paid according to distribution windows, with different rates for each window (e.g., network, syndication, streaming).

12. **Buyouts**: In some cases, actors may agree to a buyout, where they receive a lump sum payment upfront in exchange for waiving future residuals.

13. **Filing Claims**: Actors must track their work and file residual claims with the appropriate union or guild to ensure they receive payment for their performances.

14. **Residuals Departments**: Many studios and production companies have residuals departments responsible for processing and distributing residual payments.

15. **Payment Timing**: Residual payments are typically made on a quarterly basis, with specific deadlines for filing claims.

16. **Royalty Pools**: Some projects have royalty pools, where a percentage of revenue is set aside for residual payments to all participants, including actors.

17. **Duration of Residuals**: Residuals are paid for a specified period or number of airings, depending on the terms of the actor's contract and union agreements.

18. **Negotiating Power**: Actors with more leverage, such as established stars or lead roles, may have more negotiating power to secure favorable residual terms in their contracts.

19. **Passive Income**: Residuals provide actors with a form of passive income, allowing them to earn money from past work while pursuing new projects.

20. **Importance of Understanding Contracts**: It's crucial for actors to understand the terms of their contracts, including residual provisions, to ensure they receive fair compensation for their contributions to television and film projects.

By understanding the intricacies of television

and film residuals, actors can better navigate

their careers and advocate for fair compensation

for their work in the industry.

Please remember that each audition is a

chance to learn and grow so approach

them with enthusiasm and a willingness

to improve.

Good Luck & See Resources Below!

SPOTLIGHT SUCCESS

TECHNIQUES &

SELF CHECKLIST:

WAIT!! FIIIIIIRRRRRST!!!

Are you healthy, ready & available? This business takes energy!

Regular exercise for all walks of life offers a multitude of benefits for both physical and mental well-being.

Here are 20 benefits of working out:

1. **Improved Cardiovascular Health:** Regular exercise strengthens the heart, improves circulation, and reduces the risk of heart disease and stroke.

2. **Weight Management:** Exercise helps control weight by burning calories and increasing metabolism, making it easier to maintain a healthy body weight.

3. **Increased Muscle Strength and Endurance:** Strength training exercises build muscle mass and improve muscle endurance, leading to better overall strength and functional abilities.

4. **Enhanced Flexibility:** Stretching exercises improve flexibility, range of motion, and joint mobility, reducing the risk of injury and enhancing athletic performance.

5. **Better Bone Health:** Weight-bearing exercises such as walking, running, and weightlifting help build and maintain bone density, reducing the risk of osteoporosis.

6. **Improved Balance and Coordination:** Exercise improves balance and coordination, reducing the risk of falls and enhancing overall stability.

7. **Reduced Risk of Chronic Diseases:** Regular physical activity lowers the risk of developing chronic conditions such as type 2 diabetes, hypertension, and certain types of cancer.

8. **Boosted Immune System:** Exercise strengthens the immune system, making it more resilient to infections and reducing the severity and duration of illness.

9. **Enhanced Mental Health:** Exercise releases endorphins, neurotransmitters that promote feelings of happiness and reduce stress, anxiety, and depression.

10. **Improved Cognitive Function:** Regular physical activity improves memory, concentration, and cognitive function, reducing the risk of cognitive decline and dementia as you age.

11. **Better Sleep Quality:** Exercise promotes better sleep by regulating sleep-wake cycles, reducing insomnia, and improving sleep duration and quality.

12. **Increased Energy Levels:** Regular physical activity boosts energy levels, reduces fatigue, and improves overall vitality and stamina.

13. **Stress Relief:** Exercise serves as a natural stress reliever, helping to alleviate tension, improve mood, and promote relaxation.

14. **Enhanced Self-Esteem:** Achieving fitness goals and feeling stronger and more confident in your body can boost self-esteem and body image.

15. **Social Interaction:** Participating in group exercise classes or team sports provides opportunities for social interaction, support, and camaraderie.

16. **Improved Posture:** Strengthening core muscles and improving flexibility can help correct poor posture and reduce back pain.

17. **Increased Longevity:** Regular exercise is associated with a longer lifespan and a higher quality of life in older adults.

18. **Better Digestive Health:** Moderate exercise can aid in digestion, reduce constipation, and improve overall gastrointestinal health.

19. **Enhanced Circulation:** Exercise improves circulation and increases stamina leading to a more satisfying life.

20. **Sense of Achievement:** Setting and achieving fitness goals whether it's running a marathon or mastering a new yoga pose, provides a sense of accomplishment and motivation.

These benefits highlight the importance of incorporating regular exercise into your lifestyle for optimal physical and mental health.

Whether it's through structured workouts, sports, or recreational activities, finding activities you enjoy can make exercise a sustainable and enjoyable part of your routine.

SKIN (Complexion??)

Maintaining skin health involves a combination of

skincare practices, lifestyle choices and dietary

habits.

Here are 20 ways to keep your skin healthy: 1. **Protect from Sun Exposure:** Wear sunscreen with at least SPF 30 daily, even on cloudy days, and reapply every two hours when outdoors.

2. **Stay Hydrated:** Drink plenty of water throughout the day to keep your skin hydrated and maintain its elasticity.

3. **Follow a Consistent Skincare Routine:** Cleanse, tone, moisturize, and use treatments suitable for your skin type twice daily.

4. **Eat a Balanced Diet:** Consume a diet rich in fruits, vegetables, lean proteins, and healthy fats to provide essential nutrients for skin health.

5. **Limit Sugar and Processed Foods:** Reduce consumption of sugary snacks and processed foods, as they can contribute to inflammation and skin issues.

6. **Get Adequate Sleep:** Aim for 7-9 hours of quality sleep each night to allow your skin time to repair and regenerate.

7. **Manage Stress:** Practice stress-reducing activities such as meditation, yoga, or deep breathing exercises to prevent stress-related skin problems.

8. **Exercise Regularly:** Physical activity improves circulation, which nourishes skin cells and helps flush out toxins through sweating.

9. **Avoid Smoking:** Smoking accelerates skin aging by damaging collagen and elastin fibers, leading to wrinkles and sagging skin.

10. **Cleanse Makeup Brushes:** Clean makeup brushes regularly to prevent the buildup of bacteria that can cause breakouts and infections.

11. **Moisturize Daily:** Use a moisturizer suited to your skin type to keep your skin hydrated and prevent dryness and irritation.

12. **Exfoliate Weekly:** Gently exfoliate your skin 1-2 times a week to remove dead skin cells and promote cell turnover for a brighter complexion.

13. **Use Gentle Products:** Choose skincare products free of harsh chemicals and fragrances that can irritate sensitive skin.

14. **Protect Lips:** Apply a lip balm with SPF to protect your lips from sun damage and keep them moisturized.

15. **Avoid Hot Showers:** Hot water can strip the skin of its natural oils, leading to dryness and irritation. Opt for lukewarm water instead.

16. **Change Pillowcases Regularly:** Clean pillowcases prevent the buildup of bacteria and oil transfer, reducing the risk of breakouts.

17. **Stay Consistent with Medications:** If you have a skin condition requiring medication, such as acne or eczema, follow your dermatologist's recommendations consistently.

18. **Hydrate from Within:** Eat water-rich foods like cucumbers, watermelon, and oranges to hydrate your skin from the inside out.

19. **Protect Skin in Cold Weather:** Use a rich moisturizer and wear protective clothing to shield your skin from cold, windy conditions.

20. **Visit a Dermatologist:** Schedule regular check-ups with a dermatologist to monitor your skin's health and address any concerns promptly.

OTHER THINGS:

Improving skin complexion can involve a variety of approaches, from skincare products to lifestyle changes. Here are five extremely different things you can use to help your skin complexion:

1. Sunscreen: One of the most important things you can use to protect and improve your skin complexion is sunscreen.

Regularly applying a broad-spectrum sunscreen with SPF 30 or higher helps to shield your skin from harmful UV rays, preventing sunburn, premature aging, and reducing the risk of skin cancer. Choose a sunscreen that suits your skin type and apply it generously to all exposed areas of skin, especially when spending time outdoors.

2. Hydration: Drinking an adequate amount of water is essential for maintaining hydrated and healthy-looking skin. Proper hydration helps to flush out toxins, regulate oil production, and improve skin elasticity and texture. Aim to drink at least 8 glasses of water per day, and consider incorporating hydrating foods such as fruits, vegetables, and herbal teas into your diet to support overall skin health.

3. Exfoliation: Exfoliating your skin regularly helps to remove dead skin cells, unclog pores, and promote cell turnover, resulting in a brighter and more even complexion. Choose a gentle exfoliating scrub or chemical exfoliant suitable for your skin type, and use it 1-3 times per week to reveal smoother, radiant skin underneath. Be cautious not to over-exfoliate, as it can lead to irritation and sensitivity.

4. Topical treatments: Incorporating topical treatments such as serums, creams, or masks into your skincare routine can target specific skin concerns and improve complexion. Look for products containing ingredients like vitamin C, retinol, hyaluronic acid, niacinamide, or botanical extracts known for their antioxidant, anti-inflammatory, hydrating, or brightening properties. Consult with a dermatologist or skincare professional to determine the best products for your skin type and concerns.

5. Stress Management: Managing stress levels is crucial for maintaining healthy skin complexion. Chronic stress can lead to increased inflammation, breakouts, and dullness in the skin. Practice stress-reducing techniques such as mindfulness meditation, deep breathing exercises, yoga, or engaging in hobbies and activities you enjoy. Prioritize self-care and take time to relax and unwind regularly to support overall skin health and well-being.

By incorporating these different approaches into your skincare routine and lifestyle, you can help improve your skin complexion and achieve a healthy glowing appearance.

By incorporating these habits into your daily routine

you can maintain healthy glowing skin at any age.

Remember that consistency is key and it may take

time to see noticeable improvements.

Dental

The Importance of a Healthy Smile for Models and Actors

As a model or actor, it's crucial to have a bright and healthy smile. While there are various types of smiles, including those with gaps or unique features, the main focus should always be on maintaining good oral health.

Here are 20 things you can do to take care of your teeth and maintain a confident smile:

1. **Brush Your Teeth Twice Daily:** Brush your teeth in the morning and before bed using fluoride toothpaste to remove plaque and prevent cavities.

2. **Floss Daily:** Flossing helps remove plaque and food particles from between your teeth and along the gum line, where your toothbrush may not reach.

3. **Use Mouthwash:** Rinse with an antimicrobial mouthwash to kill bacteria, freshen your breath, and maintain oral hygiene.

4. **Visit Your Dentist Regularly:** Schedule dental check-ups and cleanings every six months to monitor your oral health and address any issues promptly.

5. **Address Dental Issues Promptly:** If you experience tooth pain, sensitivity, or other dental problems, don't ignore them. See your dentist as soon as possible for treatment.

6. **Avoid Smoking and Tobacco Products:** Smoking and using tobacco can stain your teeth, cause gum disease, and increase the risk of oral cancer.

7. **Limit Sugary Foods and Beverages:** Sugary foods and drinks can contribute to tooth decay and cavities. Limit your intake and brush your teeth after consuming them.

8. **Drink Plenty of Water:** Water helps wash away food particles and bacteria from your mouth, preventing dry mouth and reducing the risk of cavities.

9. **Chew Sugar-Free Gum:** Chewing sugar-free gum stimulates saliva production, which helps neutralize acids in your mouth and prevent tooth decay.

10. **Protect Your Teeth During Sports:** If you participate in contact sports, wear a mouth guard to protect your teeth from injury.

11. **Avoid Using Teeth as Tools:** Don't use your teeth to open packages, tear tags, or bite on hard objects, as this can damage your teeth.

12. **Use a Soft-Bristled Toothbrush:** Choose a toothbrush with soft bristles to avoid damaging your tooth enamel and gums while brushing.

13. **Brush Your Tongue:** Gently brush your tongue to remove bacteria and freshen your breath.

14. **Consider Teeth Whitening:** If you're concerned about tooth discoloration, talk to your dentist about professional teeth whitening options to brighten your smile.

15. **Practice Good Nutrition:** Eat a balanced diet rich in fruits, vegetables, lean proteins, and dairy products to support overall oral health.

16. **Be Mindful of Teeth Grinding:** If you grind your teeth at night, consider wearing a night guard to protect your teeth from damage.

17. **Stay Hydrated:** Drinking water throughout the day helps maintain saliva production, which is essential for oral health.

18. **Practice Good Oral Hygiene Habits:** Teach yourself good oral hygiene habits and make them a regular part of your daily routine.

19. **Limit Acidic Foods and Drinks:** Acidic foods and beverages can erode tooth enamel.

Limit your intake and rinse your mouth with water afterward.

20. **Smile with Confidence:** A confident smile is your best accessory as a model or actor.

Take pride in your oral health and smile with confidence on and off the camera.

Several factors can

contribute to staining or

discoloration of teeth:

1. **Food and Beverages**: Certain foods and beverages contain pigments that can stain teeth over time. Examples include coffee, tea, red wine, berries, and highly pigmented sauces like tomato sauce and soy sauce.

2. **Tobacco Use**: Both smoking and smokeless tobacco can stain teeth. Nicotine and tar in tobacco products can leave yellow or brown stains on teeth, which can become more pronounced over time with continued use.

3. **Poor Oral Hygiene**: Inadequate brushing and flossing can allow plaque and tartar to build up on teeth, leading to discoloration. Plaque can absorb stains from food and beverages, making teeth appear yellow or discolored.

4. **Aging**: As you age, the outer layer of enamel on your teeth naturally wears away, revealing the yellowish dentin underneath. This can make teeth appear more yellow or discolored with age.

5. **Medications**: Certain medications, such as tetracycline antibiotics, can cause tooth discoloration when taken during tooth development (in childhood). Other medications, such as antihistamines and antipsychotics, can cause staining as a side effect.

6. **Genetics**: Some people are more prone to tooth discoloration due to genetic factors. For example, some individuals may naturally have thinner enamel, making the underlying dentin more visible and teeth appear more yellow.

7. **Trauma**: Trauma to the teeth, such as a fall or injury, can cause the teeth to become discolored. This may be due to internal bleeding within the tooth or the deposition of materials from the bloodstream into the tooth structure.

Overall, practicing good oral hygiene, avoiding tobacco use, and limiting consumption of staining foods and beverages can help prevent or reduce tooth discoloration. Regular dental cleanings can also remove surface stains and help keep your teeth looking their best.

By incorporating these dental care tips into your daily

routine you can maintain a healthy and radiant smile that

enhances your overall appearance as a model or actor.

NICE WORK!! OK, now that we have gone over a few

things and done a self check let's get started from home

first

STARTING AT HOME

Starting a modeling and acting

career from home can be

challenging but not impossible.

Here are 50 ways you can kick start your journey from the comfort of your own home:

1. **Research the Industry**: Spend time researching the modeling and acting industry to understand its various facets, requirements and opportunities.

2. **Create a Plan**: Develop a strategic plan outlining your goals, timeline and steps to achieve them.

3. **Set Up a Home Studio**: Create a designated space in your home for practicing monologues, recording self-tapes and taking photos.

4. **Practice Acting Skills**: Dedicate time each day to practice acting techniques, character development and script analysis.

5. **Practice Posing**: Work on your posing skills by practicing different poses in front of a mirror or camera.

6. **Improve Speaking Skills**: Practice speaking clearly and confidently by reading scripts aloud or recording yourself speaking.

7. **Take Online Classes**: Enroll in online acting classes or workshops to improve your skills and gain industry knowledge.

8. **Watch Tutorials**: Watch tutorials and instructional videos on acting techniques, audition tips and modeling poses.

9. **Build Confidence**: Work on building your confidence through daily affirmations, visualization exercises and positive self-talk.

10. **Create a Portfolio**: Develop a digital portfolio showcasing your best photos, headshots and self-tapes.

11. **Learn Makeup Techniques**: Experiment with makeup techniques for different looks and characters.

12. **Network Online**: Join online communities, forums, and social media groups related to acting and modeling to connect with industry professionals and peers.

13. **Create a Website or Blog**: Start a website or blog to showcase your work, share industry insights and attract potential clients and collaborators.

14. **Attend Virtual Events**: Participate in virtual workshops, seminars and networking events to expand your knowledge and network.

15. **Collaborate with Others**: Collaborate with photographers, makeup artists and other creatives on virtual shoots and projects.

16. **Submit to Online Casting Calls**: Use online casting platforms to submit your portfolio for virtual auditions and modeling gigs.

17. **Build a Social Media Presence**: Establish a strong presence on social media platforms like Instagram, TikTok and YouTube to showcase your talent and attract followers.

18. **Engage with Followers**: Interact with your audience by responding to comments, sharing behind-the-scenes content and posting regularly.

19. **Create Self-Tapes**: Practice creating self-tape auditions for acting roles and modeling submissions.

20. **Study Industry Trends**: Stay up-to-date on industry trends, casting calls, and opportunities by following industry news and blogs.

21. **Research Management Companies**: Research modeling and talent agencies that accept online submissions and follow their submission guidelines.

22. **Take Photos**: Experiment with self-portraits and photography to create compelling images for your portfolio.

23. **Learn Editing Skills**: Familiarize yourself with basic photo and video editing software to enhance your portfolio materials.

24. **Develop a Signature Look**: Identify a signature look or style that sets you apart and makes you memorable to casting directors and agents.

25. **Practice Movement**: Practice movement exercises and dance routines to improve your physicality and expressiveness.

26. **Work on Vocal Variety**: Practice using different vocal tones, accents, and styles to expand your range as an actor.

27. **Create Character Monologues**: Write and perform character monologues to showcase your versatility and acting range.

28. **Learn about Industry Terminology**: Familiarize yourself with industry terminology, audition jargon, and technical terms used in the modeling and acting world.

29. **Attend Virtual Masterclasses**: Take advantage of virtual masterclasses and workshops offered by industry professionals to learn from experienced mentors.

30. **Research Casting Directors**: Research casting directors and their preferences to tailor your submissions and auditions to their specific needs.

31. **Practice Cold Reading**: Practice cold reading scripts to improve your ability to quickly analyze and interpret text during auditions.

32. **Volunteer for Virtual Projects**: Offer to volunteer for virtual film projects, student films or online theater productions to gain experience and exposure.

33. **Create a Reel**: Compile your best acting clips into a demo reel to showcase your talent and versatility to potential agents and casting directors.

34. **Join Online Talent Platforms**: Sign up for online talent platforms and databases where you can showcase your portfolio and connect with industry professionals.

35. **Research Online Marketplaces**: Explore online marketplaces for modeling gigs, promotional opportunities and freelance work.

36. **Write Scripts**: Practice writing scripts for short films, monologues or web series to showcase your creativity and storytelling skills.

37. **Create a Pitch Deck**: Develop a pitch deck outlining your skills, experience, and career goals to present to potential agents or collaborators.

38. **Learn about Self-Marketing**: Educate yourself on self-marketing strategies, branding, and personal promotion to effectively market yourself as a talent.

39. **Seek Feedback**: Seek feedback on your work from mentors, peers and industry professionals to identify areas for improvement and growth.

40. **Practice Audition Etiquette**: Familiarize yourself with audition etiquette, including how to slate, dress appropriately and conduct yourself during auditions.

41. **Create Online Workshops or Classes**: Consider offering online workshops or classes in acting, modeling or related skills to share your knowledge and generate income.

42. **Participate in Virtual Competitions**: Enter virtual talent competitions or contests to gain exposure and recognition for your talent.

43. **Stay Informed**: Stay informed about industry news, events, and opportunities by subscribing to industry newsletters, blogs and podcasts.

44. **Collaborate on Virtual Projects**: Collaborate with other actors, filmmakers, and creatives on virtual projects such as short films, web series or online performances.

45. **Learn about Contracts and Negotiation**: Educate yourself on contract terms, negotiation strategies and industry standards for talent agreements.

46. **Create Educational Content**: Share your expertise by creating educational content such as tutorials, how-to guides or industry insights on social media or your website.

47. **Attend Virtual Audition Workshops**: Participate in virtual audition workshops or classes to improve your audition skills and techniques.

48. **Offer Virtual Coaching Services**: Consider offering virtual coaching or mentoring services for aspiring actors and models looking to learn from your experience.

49. **Stay Inspired**: Surround yourself with inspiration by watching films, TV shows, theater performances and other creative works that motivate and energize you.

50. **Stay Persistent and Patient**: Building a career in modeling and acting takes time, dedication, and perseverance. Stay persistent, patient, and resilient in pursuing your goals and celebrate every milestone along the way.

By implementing these strategies and staying proactive you can start your modeling and acting career from home and lay the foundation for future success in the industry.

FACIAL EXPRESSIONS

Working on facial expressions is essential for

actors to effectively convey emotions and

connect with their audience.

Here are 50 things actors can do to improve their facial expressions:

1. Practice in front of a mirror to observe and refine facial movements.

2. Study photographs of various emotions and try to replicate them.

3. Experiment with exaggerating expressions to understand their range.

4. Watch films or TV shows with skilled actors and analyze their facial expressions.

5. Take acting classes or workshops that focus on expression and emotion.

6. Practice mindfulness to become more aware of your own facial reactions.

7. Use props or visual cues to trigger specific emotions and expressions.

8. Practice relaxation techniques to keep facial muscles loose and expressive.

9. Study facial anatomy to understand how muscles work together to create expressions.

10. Practice facial warm-up exercises before rehearsals or performances.

11. Work on controlling micro-expressions, subtle, fleeting facial expressions that convey emotions.

12. Practice expressing emotions without relying on words.

13. Record yourself practicing scenes and analyze your facial expressions.

14. Experiment with different techniques for expressing the same emotion.

15. Work with a partner or coach who can give feedback on your expressions.

16. Practice transitioning smoothly between different emotions.

17. Explore the connection between your character's inner thoughts and outward expressions.

18. Use improvisation exercises to practice spontaneous facial reactions.

19. Practice maintaining eye contact while expressing emotions.

20. Study different cultural expressions and gestures to broaden your range.

21. Experiment with using your entire face, including eyes, eyebrows, mouth, and cheeks.

22. Practice expressing emotions with different levels of intensity.

23. Use visualization techniques to imagine scenarios that evoke specific emotions.

24. Practice expressing emotions while speaking lines or monologues.

25. Experiment with incorporating physical movement into your facial expressions.

26. Study famous paintings or sculptures to observe how artists depict emotions.

27. Practice expressing emotions in front of a camera to get comfortable with on-screen work.

28. Work on maintaining authenticity and sincerity in your expressions.

29. Experiment with facial expressions in everyday situations, such as conversations with friends or family.

30. Practice expressing emotions with variations in timing and pacing.

31. Use music as inspiration to evoke specific emotions and expressions.

32. Practice expressing emotions with different levels of subtlety.

33. Work on expressing emotions non-verbally while listening to others speak.

34. Practice expressing conflicting or complex emotions simultaneously.

35. Experiment with using props or costumes to enhance your expressions.

36. Study different acting techniques that emphasize the importance of facial expression.

37. Practice expressing emotions while maintaining character objectives and intentions.

38. Work on expressing emotions authentically without overacting.

39. Practice expressing emotions in different environments and contexts.

40. Experiment with expressing emotions in different genres, such as comedy, drama, or horror.

41. Use sensory exercises to evoke emotions that naturally translate into facial expressions.

42. Practice expressing emotions in close-up shots to focus on subtle facial nuances.

43. Work on expressing emotions with consistency throughout a scene or performance.

44. Practice expressing emotions in front of a live audience to gauge reactions.

45. Use props or imagery to evoke specific memories and emotions.

46. Experiment with using facial expressions to convey subtext and underlying emotions.

47. Practice expressing emotions while incorporating vocal variations.

48. Work on expressing emotions with authenticity and vulnerability.

49. Seek feedback from peers, instructors, or directors on your facial expressions.

50. Practice regularly and be patient with yourself – improving facial expressions takes time and dedication.

By incorporating these practices into their routine, actors can develop

more nuanced, authentic, and compelling facial expressions to

enhance their performances.

EMOTIONS

Here are 50 techniques and exercises actors can use to tap into different emotions:

1. **Emotional Memory:** Recall personal experiences that evoke the desired emotion.

2. **Sense Memory:** Focus on sensory details associated with past emotional experiences.

3. **Imagination:** Create vivid mental images or scenarios to stimulate emotional responses.

4. **Substitution:** Relate the character's circumstances to personal experiences or feelings.

5. **Physical Warm-Up:** Engage in physical exercises to prepare the body for emotional work.

6. **Breath Work:** Use controlled breathing techniques to regulate emotions.

7. **Voice Work:** Explore how changes in vocal tone and quality affect emotional expression.

8. **Character Analysis:** Understand the character's backstory, motivations, and emotional arc.

9. **Journaling:** Write from the character's perspective to delve into their emotions.

10. **Improvisation:** React spontaneously to given circumstances to access authentic emotions.

11. **Script Analysis:** Identify key emotional beats and transitions within the text.

12. **Emotional Preparation:** Mentally and emotionally prepare before rehearsals or performances.

13. **Meditation:** Practice mindfulness to become more aware of emotional states.

14. **Music:** Listen to music that evokes the desired emotion to get into the right mindset.

15. **Physical Gesture:** Use specific physical gestures or movements associated with the emotion.

16. **Animal Study:** Observe and mimic animal behavior associated with the emotion.

17. **Image Work:** Visualize symbolic images or scenes related to the emotion.

18. **Object Work:** Interact with objects that evoke emotional associations.

19. **Partner Exercises:** Engage in emotional exchanges with scene partners to trigger responses.

20. **Monologue Work:** Explore monologues that resonate with the desired emotion.

21. **Role Play:** Assume the persona of someone who naturally experiences the emotion.

22. **Character Interviews:** Answer questions as the character to delve into their emotional landscape.

23. **Sensory Exploration:** Engage all five senses to fully immerse in the emotional experience.

24. **Psychological Analysis:** Understand the psychological underpinnings of the emotion.

25. **Movement Exploration:** Experiment with different physical movements to express the emotion.

26. **Rehearsal Techniques:** Practice scenes repeatedly to deepen emotional connections.

27. **Environment Study:** Explore how different settings affect emotional states.

28. **Empathy Exercises:** Put yourself in another person's shoes to understand their emotions.

29. **Psychodrama:** Act out past experiences or conflicts to release pent-up emotions.

30. **Guided Imagery:** Follow guided scripts to visualize scenarios that evoke specific emotions.

31. **Physical Contact:** Engage in physical contact or touch to stimulate emotional responses.

32. **Character Study:** Research historical or fictional figures known for experiencing the emotion.

33. **Situational Analysis:** Consider how external factors influence emotional responses.

34. **Dream Work:** Reflect on dreams or nightmares that tap into the desired emotion.

35. **Movement Therapy:** Use dance or movement exercises to express and release emotions.

36. **Conflict Exploration:** Investigate internal and external conflicts that fuel the emotion.

37. **Cognitive Behavioral Techniques:** Challenge and reframe thoughts to influence emotions.

38. **Personalization:** Find personal connections to the character's circumstances and emotions.

39. **Regression Therapy:** Explore childhood memories or traumas related to the emotion.

40. **Archetype Study:** Connect with universal symbols and patterns associated with the emotion.

41. **Role Reversal:** Switch roles with another actor to gain perspective on emotional dynamics.

42. **Symbolism:** Work with symbolic objects or images to represent the emotion metaphorically.

43. **Artistic Expression:** Engage in other art forms (painting, writing, etc.) to process emotions.

44. **Improv Games:** Play games that encourage spontaneity and emotional exploration.

45. **Regression Techniques:** Tap into childlike innocence or vulnerability to access emotions.

46. **Character Diary:** Write diary entries from the character's perspective to explore emotions.

47. **Mask Work:** Use masks or facial expressions to externalize and exaggerate emotions.

48. **Bioenergetics:** Release emotional blocks through physical exercises and movement.

49. **Shadow Work:** Confront and integrate suppressed or hidden emotions.

50. **Self-Reflection:** Regularly assess and evaluate emotional progress and growth as an actor.

By incorporating these techniques into

their practice, actors can deepen their

MOTIVATION

If you find yourself feeling lazy or

daydreaming and want to snap out of

it here are 20 strategies to help you

regain focus and motivation:

Come on people!! Take notes!!

L.O.L.....How much does it mean to

you???

1. **Set Clear Goals:** Define specific, achievable goals for the day or week to give yourself a sense of purpose and direction.

2. **Break Tasks into Smaller Steps:** Divide larger tasks into smaller, manageable steps to make them feel less overwhelming and easier to tackle.

3. **Create a To-Do List:** Write down your tasks and prioritize them. Checking off items as you complete them can provide a sense of accomplishment and motivation.

4. **Set a Timer:** Use the Pomodoro Technique or similar methods to work in focused intervals with short breaks in between to prevent burnout.

5. **Change Your Environment:** Move to a different location, such as a coffee shop or library to change your surroundings and stimulate your mind.

6. **Listen to Upbeat Music:** Play energetic music that motivates you and helps you stay focused on your tasks.

7. **Practice Mindfulness:** Take a few minutes to practice mindfulness or deep breathing exercises to calm your mind and increase your focus.

8. **Visualize Success:** Imagine yourself completing your tasks successfully and visualize the positive outcomes of your efforts.

9. **Reward Yourself:** Set up rewards for completing tasks or reaching milestones to create positive reinforcement and motivation.

10. **Limit Distractions:** Identify and minimize distractions such as social media, emails, or noisy environments that can derail your focus.

11. **Get Moving:** Engage in physical activity or take a short walk to increase your energy levels and stimulate your mind.

12. **Stay Hydrated:** Drink water regularly throughout the day to stay hydrated, which can help maintain focus and prevent fatigue.

13. **Practice Self-Discipline:** Remind yourself of the importance of staying focused and disciplined, even when you don't feel like it.

14. **Find Inspiration:** Surround yourself with inspirational quotes, books, or videos that motivate you to take action and pursue your goals.

15. **Seek Accountability:** Share your goals with a friend, family member, or colleague who can hold you accountable and provide support.

16. **Take Breaks Strategically:** Schedule short breaks throughout your work sessions to prevent burnout and maintain productivity.

17. **Challenge Negative Thoughts:** Challenge negative self-talk and replace it with positive affirmations to boost your confidence and motivation.

18. **Set Deadlines:** Establish deadlines for your tasks to create a sense of urgency and prevent procrastination.

19. **Visual Cues:** Place visual cues or reminders around your workspace to keep you focused on your goals and tasks.

20. **Reflect on Progress:** Take time to reflect on your progress and celebrate your achievements, no matter how small, to stay motivated and maintain momentum.

Using these strategies can help you snap out of laziness or daydreaming and refocus your energy on achieving your goals and tasks.

Experiment with different techniques to find what works best for you and incorporate them into your daily routine.

CONFIDENCE

Building confidence is a gradual

process that involves both mindset

shifts and practical actions.

Here are 20 ways to help build your confidence: 1. **Set Realistic Goals:** Break down your larger goals into smaller, achievable steps. Each accomplishment will boost your confidence.

2. **Practice Self-Compassion:** Treat yourself with kindness and understanding, especially during setbacks or failures.

3. **Celebrate Your Achievements:** Acknowledge and celebrate even the smallest victories to reinforce positive feelings about yourself.

4. **Challenge Negative Self-Talk:** Pay attention to your inner dialogue and challenge negative thoughts with evidence-based positive affirmations.

5. **Focus on Strengths:** Identify your strengths and talents, and focus on developing and showcasing them.

6. **Step Out of Your Comfort Zone:** Push yourself to try new things, even if they scare you.

Growth happens outside of your comfort zone.

7. **Practice Visualization:** Visualize yourself succeeding and feeling confident in various situations to mentally prepare yourself.

8. **Improve Your Posture:** Standing tall with good posture can make you feel more confident and powerful.

9. **Dress for Success:** Wear clothes that make you feel comfortable and confident. When you look good, you feel good.

10. **Learn New Skills:** Investing in learning and acquiring new skills can boost your confidence and self-esteem.

11. **Seek Feedback:** Ask for feedback from trusted friends, mentors, or coaches to gain insight into your strengths and areas for improvement.

12. **Surround Yourself with Positive Influences:** Spend time with supportive and encouraging people who uplift you and believe in your abilities.

13. **Practice Gratitude:** Reflect on the things you're grateful for in your life. Gratitude can help shift your focus from what you lack to what you have.

14. **Stay Present:** Focus on the present moment rather than worrying about the past or future. Mindfulness can help reduce anxiety and boost confidence.

15. **Help Others:** Volunteering or helping others can boost your self-esteem and sense of purpose.

16. **Take Care of Your Physical Health:** Regular exercise, proper nutrition, and adequate sleep can improve your mood and overall well-being, contributing to greater confidence.

17. **Set Boundaries:** Learn to say no to things that drain your energy or undermine your confidence. Prioritize activities that align with your values and goals.

18. **Keep Learning and Growing:** Embrace a growth mindset and view challenges as opportunities for learning and personal development.

19. **Practice Assertiveness:** Communicate your needs and desires clearly and respectfully, without being passive or aggressive.

20. **Reflect on Your Progress:** Regularly assess your progress and celebrate how far you've come on your journey to building confidence.

OTHER THINGS:

Building confidence can be a unique journey for everyone, but here are five unusual strategies

you can try:

*1. **Power Posing**: Strike a power pose for a few minutes before a challenging situation.*

Research suggests that adopting expansive postures, such as standing with your feet apart and

your hands on your hips (like Wonder Woman), can increase feelings of power and confidence.

*2. **Try Improv or Acting Classes**: Participating in improv or acting classes can help you break*

out of your comfort zone, improve your communication skills, and become more comfortable with

spontaneity and uncertainty. These skills can translate to increased confidence in various social

and professional settings.

*3. **Challenge Your Comfort Zone Regularly**: Make a habit of intentionally doing things that*

scare you or make you uncomfortable. This could be anything from striking up a conversation

with a stranger to trying a new hobby or activity. Each time you step outside your comfort zone and succeed, you'll build confidence in your abilities.

4. **Practice Positive Self-Talk in Front of a Mirror**: Stand in front of a mirror and practice

affirmations or positive self-talk aloud. Speak to yourself as you would to a friend, focusing on

your strengths, accomplishments, and potential. This exercise can help reframe negative

self-perceptions and boost self-confidence.

5. **Document Your Achievements in a "Brag Book"**: Create a "brag book" or digital folder where

you compile evidence of your accomplishments, praises, and positive feedback you've received

from others. Whenever you're feeling doubtful or insecure, flip through your brag book to remind

yourself of your capabilities and past successes.

Remember that building confidence is an ongoing process, so be patient and kind to yourself as

you explore these strategies and find what works best for you.

FEAR?.... STAGE FRIGHT???

Overcoming the fear of being an entertainer can be

a challenging but rewarding journey.

Here are 20 strategies to help you conquer that fear: 1. **Identify the Root Cause:** Understand what specifically about being an entertainer triggers fear. Is it fear of failure, rejection, or stage fright?

2. **Positive Visualization**: Visualize yourself performing confidently and successfully. This can help rewire your brain to associate positive outcomes with being an entertainer.

3. **Set Realistic Goals**: Break down your journey into smaller, achievable goals. Each accomplishment will boost your confidence.

4. **Practice, Practice, Practice**: The more you rehearse your craft, the more comfortable and confident you'll become.

5. **Start Small**: Begin by performing in front of friends, family, or small audiences to ease into the experience.

6. **Focus on the Audience**: Shift your focus away from yourself and onto the enjoyment and satisfaction you bring to your audience.

7. **Learn from Others**: Study successful entertainers and observe how they handle nerves and setbacks.

8. **Join a Community**: Surround yourself with supportive peers who understand the challenges of being an entertainer.

9. **Take Acting or Public Speaking Classes**: These can provide valuable tools and techniques for managing stage fright and building confidence.

10. **Mindfulness and Breathing Exercises**: Practice mindfulness and deep breathing techniques to calm your nerves before performances.

11. **Challenge Negative Thoughts**: Replace negative self-talk with positive affirmations and realistic self-appraisals.

12. **Embrace Imperfection**: Understand that mistakes are a natural part of growth and development. Don't let fear of imperfection hold you back.

13. **Build a Support System**: Seek encouragement from friends, family, mentors, or a therapist who can provide guidance and reassurance.

14. **Expose Yourself Gradually**: Gradually expose yourself to situations that trigger fear, increasing exposure over time as you build resilience.

15. **Focus on Process Not Outcome**: Concentrate on the joy of performing rather than fixating on external validation or success.

16. **Use Humor**: Inject humor into your performances to lighten the mood and connect with your audience on a more personal level.

17. **Record and Review Performances**: Analyze your performances objectively to identify areas for improvement and celebrate your progress.

18. **Develop a pre-performance routine**: Establish a routine that helps you relax and mentally prepare before taking the stage.

19. **Seek Professional Help if Needed**: If fear significantly impacts your ability to perform, consider seeking guidance from a therapist or counselor.

20. **Celebrate Your Achievements**: Acknowledge and celebrate every step forward, no matter how small. Recognize your bravery in facing your fears head-on.

Overcoming fear often involves

gradual steps to gradually face

and manage what scares you.

Here are five steps you can take:

1. **Acknowledge Your Fear**: The first step in overcoming fear is acknowledging its presence.

Take some time to identify what specifically you're afraid of and why it's causing you distress.

This self-awareness is essential for moving forward.

2. **Break It Down**: Once you've identified your fear, break it down into smaller, more manageable steps or components. This helps make the fear seem less overwhelming and allows you to tackle it one piece at a time.

3. **Educate Yourself**: Knowledge can be empowering when facing fear. Take the time to learn more about what you're afraid of. This might involve researching the topic, seeking advice from others who have faced similar fears, or consulting with professionals who can provide guidance and support.

4. **Expose Yourself Gradually**: Exposure therapy is a common technique used to overcome fear. Start by exposing yourself to small doses of what you fear in a controlled environment. As

you become more comfortable, gradually increase the intensity or duration of exposure. This gradual approach allows you to build confidence and resilience over time.

5. **Practice Relaxation Techniques**: Learning relaxation techniques such as deep breathing, meditation, or progressive muscle relaxation can help calm your mind and body when facing fear. Practice these techniques regularly, especially before and during exposure to your fear, to help manage anxiety and increase your ability to cope.

Remember, overcoming the

fear of being an entertainer

is a gradual process.

BE PATIENT with yourself

and celebrate every victory

along the way!!!

MEMORY

Improving memory is essential for actors

and models who need to remember

lines, cues, poses and other important

details.

Here are 20 ways actors and models can enhance their memory:

1. **Rehearse Regularly:** Practice your lines, poses, or routines frequently to reinforce memory retention.

2. **Use Visualization Techniques:** Visualize the scenes, poses, or actions in your mind to create mental images that can aid memory recall.

3. **Create Mnemonics:** Develop mnemonic devices or associations to help remember lines, cues, or sequences more easily.

4. **Break Material into Chunks:** Break down long scripts or sequences into smaller, manageable chunks to make them easier to memorize.

5. **Understand the Material:** Take the time to understand the context, emotions, and motivations behind the lines or poses to make them more memorable.

6. **Practice Active Listening:** Pay close attention to cues, directions, and feedback during rehearsals and shoots to improve memory retention.

7. **Repetition:** Repeat lines, poses, or actions multiple times to reinforce memory encoding and retrieval.

8. **Use Memory Palaces:** Utilize the method of loci or memory palace technique to associate information with specific locations or visual cues.

9. **Engage Multiple Senses:** Incorporate visual, auditory, and kinesthetic cues into your rehearsal process to stimulate different sensory pathways and enhance memory.

10. **Take Breaks:** Give yourself regular breaks during rehearsals or study sessions to prevent mental fatigue and improve memory consolidation.

11. **Get Adequate Sleep:** Prioritize quality sleep to support memory consolidation and cognitive function.

12. **Stay Organized:** Keep scripts, notes, and other materials organized and easily accessible to facilitate rehearsal and memory retention.

13. **Use Memory Games:** Play memory games or puzzles to challenge and strengthen your cognitive abilities.

14. **Stay Physically Active:** Regular exercise improves blood flow to the brain, which can enhance cognitive function and memory.

15. **Maintain a Healthy Diet:** Eat a balanced diet rich in fruits, vegetables, and whole grains to provide essential nutrients that support brain health and memory.

16. **Practice Mindfulness:** Incorporate mindfulness practices such as meditation or deep breathing exercises to reduce stress and improve focus, which can enhance memory retention.

17. **Stay Hydrated:** Drink plenty of water throughout the day to support optimal brain function and memory performance.

18. **Use Memory Aids:** Carry cue cards, scripts, or prompts to refer to during rehearsals or shoots as needed.

19. **Review and Reflect:** Take time to review your performance, identify areas for improvement, and reflect on what worked well in terms of memory retention.

20. **Stay Positive:** Maintain a positive attitude and believe in your ability to improve your memory through practice and dedication.

By incorporating these memory-enhancing techniques into your rehearsal and performance routine you can improve your ability to memorize lines, poses, and other important details as an actor or model.

Acting class can really help even if you only want to be a model.

RESOURCES:

Here are the top 20 resources you may need

as a model and actor to succeed in the

industry:

1. **Portfolio/Headshots**: High-quality portfolio or headshots are essential for showcasing your versatility and attracting casting directors and agents.

2. **Model Management Company**: Joining a reputable modeling agency can provide you with access to casting calls, networking opportunities, and professional representation.

3. **Acting Classes**: Taking acting classes or workshops helps you develop your craft, improve your skills, and gain confidence in front of the camera or on stage.

4. **Audition Preparation**: Resources such as audition monologues, scripts, and scene partners can help you prepare effectively for auditions and callbacks.

5. **Networking Events**: Attending industry events, mixers, and workshops allows you to connect with other professionals in the field and build relationships that may lead to opportunities.

6. **Online Casting Platforms**: Utilize online casting platforms like Backstage, Casting Networks, or Actors Access to find and apply for auditions and casting calls.

7. **Modeling/Acting Agencies Websites**: Regularly check the websites of modeling and acting agencies for open calls, submission guidelines, and updates on industry trends and opportunities.

8. **Fitness and Nutrition Resources**: Maintaining a healthy lifestyle is crucial for models and actors. Resources such as fitness

programs, nutrition guides, and wellness coaches can help you stay in shape and look your best.

9. **Social Media Presence**: Building a strong presence on social media platforms like Instagram, TikTok, or YouTube can help you showcase your work, connect with fans, and attract industry attention.

10. **Fashion Magazines and Blogs**: Stay informed about current fashion trends, industry news, and modeling tips by reading fashion magazines and blogs.

11. **Acting Reels**: Create a professional acting reel showcasing your best performances to demonstrate your range and abilities to casting directors and agents.

12. **Voiceover Demos**: If pursuing voiceover work, record a voiceover demo highlighting your vocal range, versatility, and ability to interpret scripts.

13. **Modeling and Acting Websites**: Join online platforms dedicated to modeling and acting, where you can network with industry professionals, share your portfolio, and find job opportunities.

14. **Professional Website or Portfolio**: Create a personal website or online portfolio to showcase your work, resume, photos, and demo reels in a professional and easily accessible format.

15. **Professional Representation**: Secure professional representation by signing with a talent agent or manager who can help you find auditions, negotiate contracts, and advance your career.

16. **Industry Publications**: Subscribe to industry publications like Variety, The Hollywood Reporter, or Vogue for insights into industry trends, casting news, and success stories.

17. **Financial Planning Resources**: Learn about financial planning, budgeting, and managing your finances as a freelance model or actor to ensure stability and long-term success.

18. **Audition and Performance Apparel**: Invest in a wardrobe of appropriate attire for auditions and performances, including versatile clothing that reflects your personal style and the characters you portray.

19. **Transportation**: Reliable transportation is essential for attending auditions, castings, rehearsals, and shoots. Whether it's a car, bike, or public transit pass, make sure you have a way to get around efficiently.

20. **Professional Support System**: Surround yourself with a supportive network of friends, family, mentors, and fellow professionals who can offer encouragement, guidance, and constructive feedback throughout your modeling and acting journey.

By utilizing these resources effectively, you can enhance your skills, expand your opportunities, and build a successful career as a model and actor.

MODEL BOOK OR PORTFOLIO

A modeling portfolio is a collection of photographs or images that showcases a model's versatility, range, and unique look.

It serves as a visual representation of the model's talent, professionalism, and potential to prospective clients, agencies, and casting directors in the fashion and modeling industry.

Key components of a modeling portfolio include:

1. **Headshots**: Close-up photographs that focus on the model's face, highlighting their facial features, expressions, and personality.

2. **Full-Length Shots**: Full-body photographs that showcase the model's physique, posture, and overall proportions. These shots are often used to evaluate the model's height, body type, and posing ability.

3. **Profile Shots**: Side-view photographs that capture the model's profile, including their facial profile and body silhouette. Profile shots are useful for evaluating the model's bone structure and facial symmetry.

4. **Editorial Shots**: Fashion-forward and artistic photographs that showcase the model's ability to convey a story, mood, or concept through posing, styling, and expression. Editorial shots often feature high-fashion clothing, dramatic lighting, and creative compositions.

5. **Commercial Shots**: Images that depict the model in everyday situations or scenarios, often wearing casual clothing and portraying relatable characters. Commercial shots are versatile and suitable for a wide range of advertising and marketing campaigns.

6. **Fashion Shots**: Photographs that showcase the model wearing designer clothing, accessories, and couture fashion pieces. Fashion shots highlight the model's ability to embody the style and aesthetic of high-end fashion brands and designers.

7. **Beauty Shots**: Close-up photographs that focus on the model's hair, makeup, and beauty features. Beauty shots emphasize the model's facial symmetry, skin complexion, and grooming skills.

8. **Portfolio Layout and Presentation**: The layout and presentation of the modeling portfolio are crucial for making a strong impression. The portfolio should be well-organized,

visually appealing, and easy to navigate, with high-quality images presented in a professional manner.

9. **Digital and Print Formats**: Modeling portfolios are often available in both digital and print formats. Digital portfolios can be shared online through websites, social media, or email, while printed portfolios are used for in-person meetings, castings, and go-sees.

10. **Variety and Versatility**: A successful modeling portfolio showcases the model's versatility and ability to work in different styles, genres and settings.

Including a diverse range of photographs helps

demonstrate the model's adaptability and appeal to a wide range of clients and projects.

Overall, a modeling portfolio is a vital tool for models to market themselves and showcase their talent, professionalism, and potential to industry professionals.

It should be carefully curated and regularly updated to reflect the model's current look, skills, and experience.

HEADSHOTS

Headshots are close-up photographs of a person's face,

typically used in the entertainment industry, such as

acting, modeling, or professional networking.

These photographs serve as a visual representation of an individual and are often the first impression made on

casting directors, agents, or potential employers. Here are some key aspects of headshots:

1. **Purpose**: Headshots are used for various purposes, including audition submissions, casting calls, portfolio building, social media profiles, and professional networking platforms.

2. **Composition**: Headshots typically focus on the individual's face, shoulders, and upper torso. The composition should be clean, well-lit, and centered on the subject's face, with minimal distractions in the background.

3. **Expression**: The subject's expression in a headshot should be natural, engaging, and reflective of their personality. It's essential to convey confidence, approachability, and authenticity in the photograph.

4. **Wardrobe**: Clothing choices should be simple, flattering, and appropriate for the individual's industry or intended use of the headshot. Solid colors and classic styles are often preferred to avoid distracting from the subject's face.

5. **Hair and Makeup**: Hair and makeup should be styled in a way that enhances the subject's features without appearing overly glamorous or theatrical. Makeup should be applied subtly to enhance natural beauty and minimize shine or blemishes.

6. **Background**: The background of a headshot should be simple and unobtrusive, allowing the subject to remain the focal point. Neutral colors or blurred backgrounds are commonly used to keep the focus on the individual's face.

7. **Photographer Selection**: Choosing a skilled and experienced photographer is crucial to capturing high-quality headshots. Look for photographers who specialize in headshot photography and have a portfolio that aligns with your desired style and aesthetic.

8. **Retouching**: While some retouching may be applied to enhance the overall appearance of the headshot, it's essential to maintain a natural and authentic look. Avoid excessive retouching that alters the subject's appearance or detracts from their authenticity.

9. **Variety**: It's beneficial to have a variety of headshots that showcase different looks, expressions, and moods. This allows you to tailor your submissions to specific casting calls or professional opportunities.

10. **Digital and Print Formats**: Headshots are typically provided in both digital and print formats.

Digital headshots are commonly used for online submissions and digital

portfolios, while print headshots may be requested for physical casting calls or networking events.

Overall, headshots are an essential tool for individuals in the entertainment

industry and professional fields, serving as a visual representation of their

identity, personality, and brand. A well-executed headshot can make a

significant impact and open doors to new opportunities.

LOOKBOOK:

A Lookbook is a collection of photographs or images showcasing fashion, style, or design concepts.

It serves as a visual portfolio or catalog used by fashion designers, stylists, retailers and brands to showcase their latest collections, products, or creative ideas.

Here are some key components and purposes of a lookbook: 1. **Visual Presentation**: Lookbooks are primarily visual in nature, featuring high-quality images that highlight clothing, accessories, or design elements. The layout and design of the lookbook are carefully curated to reflect the brand's aesthetic and vision.

2. **Fashion Inspiration**: Lookbooks serve as a source of inspiration for consumers, offering ideas on how to style outfits, mix and match pieces, or incorporate current trends into their wardrobe.

3. **Product Showcase**: For fashion brands and retailers lookbooks are a way to showcase their latest collections or product lines. Each image typically features a specific item or ensemble, accompanied by details such as product names, descriptions, and prices.

4. **Brand Storytelling**: Lookbooks can help communicate the brand's identity, values, and story through imagery and styling choices. They provide an opportunity for brands to establish a unique visual identity and connect with their target audience on an emotional level.

5. **Marketing Tool**: Lookbooks are often used as marketing tools to promote new collections, seasonal trends, or special promotions. They may be distributed digitally via websites, social media platforms, or email newsletters, or printed as physical catalogs for distribution in stores or at events.

6. **Collaborations and Partnerships**: Lookbooks may feature collaborations with other brands, designers, or influencers

providing exposure and cross-promotion opportunities for all parties involved.

7. **Editorial Content**: Some lookbooks include editorial content such as styling tips, trend forecasts, or behind-the-scenes insights to engage and educate consumers.

8. **Professional Photography**: High-quality photography is essential for creating an impactful lookbook.

Professional photographers, stylists and models are often hired to ensure that the images effectively showcase the clothing or products and evoke the desired mood or aesthetic.

Overall, lookbooks serve as a versatile and effective tool for fashion brands and designers to visually communicate their creative vision, inspire consumers and drive engagement and sales.

Whether digital or printed, a well-executed lookbook can leave a lasting impression and enhance brand visibility and credibility within the fashion industry.

MONOLOGUES

https://monologueblogger.com/

YOUR WEBSITE

Some people like to have their own website with resume, stats, lookbook, headshots, commercial reel, acting reel

& anything else that will showcase their talent.

SOCIAL MEDIA:

INSTAGRAM

FACEBOOK

TIK TOK

LINKEDIN

CASTING PLATFORMS

BACKSTAGE

ACTORS ACCESS

CASTING NETWORKS

CASTING FRONTIER

CENTRAL CASTING

TEACHERS (LOS ANGELES)

IF YOU WANT TO DISCUSS THE REAL DEAL THEN IN MY

HUMBLE OPINION YOU NEED TO BE TAUGHT BY THE BEST OF

THE BEST SINCE ONLY 2% OF SAG MEMBERS ACTUALLY

MAKE A LIVING YEAR IN AND YEAR OUT!! RIGHT???

Also, in my opinion if a teacher has not personally

worked with at least 3 or 4 award winning(Academy

Award, Emmy, Golden Globe etc.)household names then

why bother Hahaha. The competition is soooo thick these

days you better be ready superstar.

Below are some Unbelievable

teachers! Yes there are others with

great credentials but I like these for

different reasons.

HOWARD FINE

MARGIE HABER

SCOTT SEDITA

IVANA CHUBBUCK

BRIAN REISE

MICHELLE DANNER

Elite acting teachers often seek specific qualities and behaviors from their students to help them excel in their craft. Here are the top 20

things they may want to see:

1. **Commitment**: Dedication and passion for the art of acting.

2. **Preparation**: Thorough preparation for each class, rehearsal, and performance.

3. **Emotional Depth**: Ability to tap into a wide range of emotions authentically.

4. **Physicality**: Utilization of body language and movement to express character emotions and intentions.

5. **Voice Control**: Mastery of vocal techniques including projection, articulation, and modulation.

6. **Listening Skills**: Capacity to actively listen and respond truthfully to scene partners.

7. **Versatility**: Willingness to explore diverse characters and genres.

8. **Character Development**: Skill in creating multidimensional characters with depth and complexity.

9. **Risk-taking**: Willingness to take creative risks and step out of one's comfort zone.

10. **Creativity**: Ability to think outside the box and bring innovative ideas to performances.

11. **Collaboration**: Ability to work effectively with directors, fellow actors, and production teams.

12. **Adaptability**: Capacity to adapt to different acting styles, techniques, and directorial approaches.

13. **Self-awareness**: Understanding of one's strengths, weaknesses, and areas for growth.

14. **Feedback Receptivity**: Openness to receiving constructive feedback and using it to improve.

15. **Persistence**: Resilience in the face of challenges and setbacks, and a commitment to continuous improvement.

16. **Empathy**: Capacity to empathize with characters and understand their motivations and emotions.

17. **Focus**: Ability to maintain concentration and stay present in the moment during scenes and performances.

18. **Authenticity**: Commitment to truthful and honest portrayals of characters and situations.

19. **Professionalism**: Conducting oneself with professionalism, punctuality, and respect for colleagues and the craft.

20. **Passion**: Genuine love for acting and storytelling, and a desire to connect with audiences on an emotional level.

Acting teachers look for these qualities and behaviors because they contribute to the development of well-rounded, skilled performers who can bring characters to life with depth, authenticity, and impact.

9 798323 828142